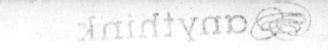

CELEBRATING HOLIDAYS

Easter

by Rachel Grack

BELLWETHER MEDIA • MINNEAPOLIS, MN

Note to Librarians, Teachers, and Parents:

Blastoff! Readers are carefully developed by literacy experts and combine standards-based content with developmentally appropriate text.

Level 1 provides the most support through repetition of high-frequency words, light text, predictable sentence patterns, and strong visual support.

Level 2 offers early readers a bit more challenge through varied simple sentences, increased text load, and less repetition of high-frequency words.

Level 3 advances early-fluent readers toward fluency through increased text and concept load, less reliance on visuals, longer sentences, and more literary language.

Level 4 builds reading stamina by providing more text per page, increased use of punctuation, greater variation in sentence patterns, and increasingly challenging vocabulary.

Level 5 encourages children to move from "learning to read" to "reading to learn" by providing even more text, varied writing styles, and less familiar topics.

Whichever book is right for your reader, Blastoff! Readers are the perfect books to build confidence and encourage a love of reading that will last a lifetime!

This edition first published in 2017 by Bellwether Media, Inc.

No part of this publication may be reproduced in whole or in part without written permission of the publisher. For information regarding permission, write to Bellwether Media, Inc., Attention: Permissions Department, 5357 Penn Avenue South, Minneapolis, MN 55419.

Library of Congress Cataloging-in-Publication Data

Names: Koestler-Grack, Rachel A., 1973- author.
Title: Easter / by Rachel Grack.
Description: Minneapolis, MN : Bellwether Media, Inc., 2017. | Series:
    Blastoff! Readers: Celebrating Holidays | Includes bibliographical
    references and index. | Audience: Ages: 5-8. | Audience: Grades: K to
    Grade 3.
Identifiers: LCCN 2016033348 (print) | LCCN 2016038620 (ebook) | ISBN
    9781626175945 (hardcover : alk. paper) | ISBN 9781681033242 (ebook)
Subjects: LCSH: Easter–Juvenile literature. | Jesus
    Christ–Resurrection–Juvenile literature.
Classification: LCC BV55 .K64 2017 (print) | LCC BV55 (ebook) | DDC
    263/.93–dc23
LC record available at https://lccn.loc.gov/2016033348

Editor: Christina Leaf   Designer: Lois Stanfield

Printed in the United States of America, North Mankato, MN.

Table of Contents

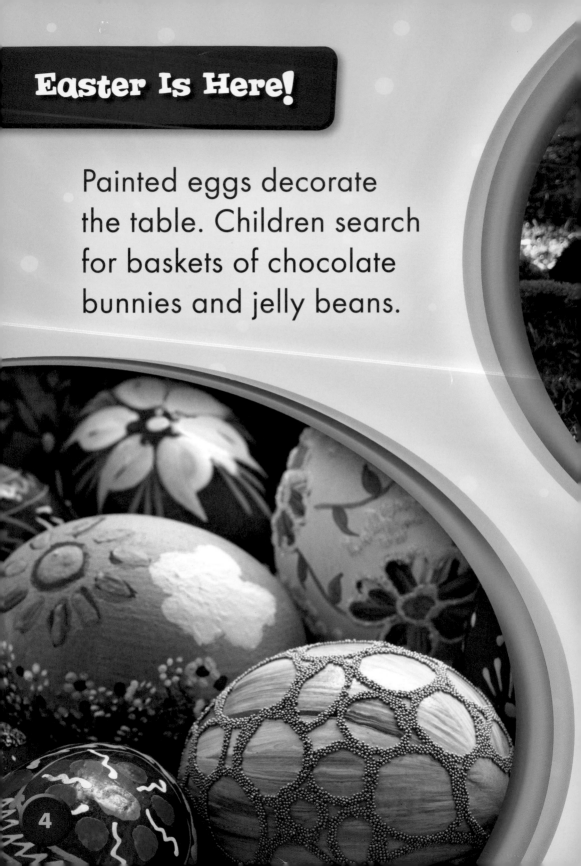

Easter Is Here!

Painted eggs decorate the table. Children search for baskets of chocolate bunnies and jelly beans.

Outside, the trees are budding.
Spring brings Easter!

What Is Easter?

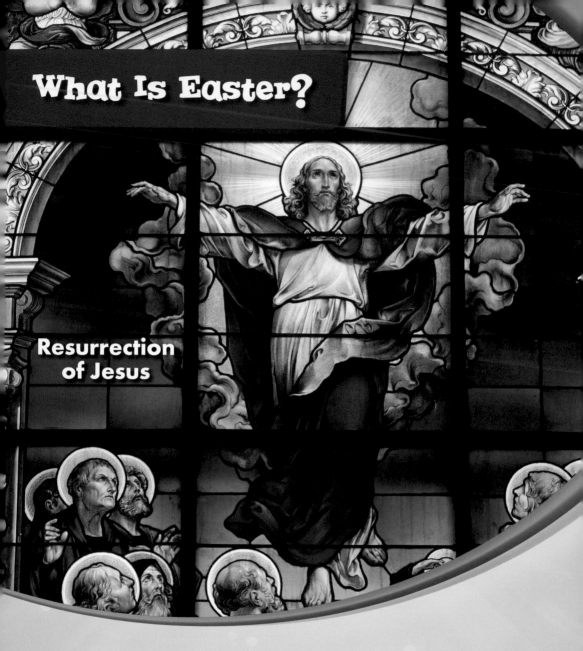

Resurrection of Jesus

Easter is an important **Christian** holiday. It celebrates the **Resurrection** of Jesus Christ.

This spring holiday also celebrates new life.

Who Celebrates Easter?

Christians all around the world celebrate Easter. Celebrations of the holiday started **centuries** ago.

Easter in Guatemala

How Do You Say Happy Easter?

Phrase	Pronunciation
French Joyeuses Pâques	JOY-yoos pack
German Frohe Ostern	FRO-ah OH-starn
Spanish Felices Pascuas	fay-LEE-sehs PASS-kwahs
Greek Καλό Πάσχα/ Kaló Páscha	kah-LOH PASS-kah

Many non-Christians enjoy Easter **traditions**, too.

The Easter story is in the **Christian Bible**. Jesus Christ was put on a cross to die near Jerusalem.

He came back to life three days later.

Israel →

West Bank →

Jerusalem →

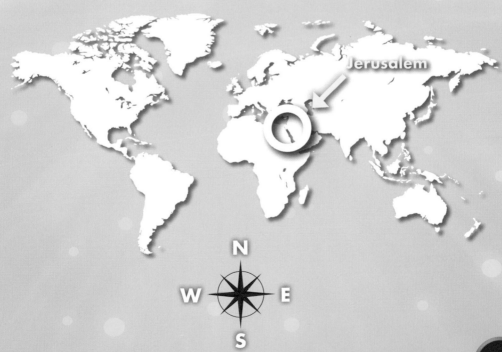

Jerusalem

N
W E
S

Followers of Jesus **rejoiced**.
They believed Jesus died to
save their souls.

They began celebrating his **victory** over death as Easter.

Time to Celebrate

Easter is on a different Sunday each year. It follows the first full moon of spring.

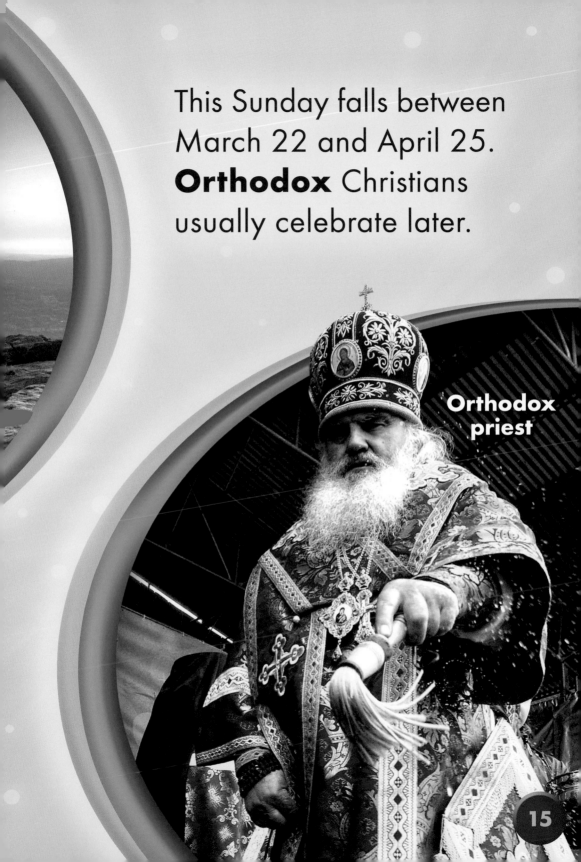

This Sunday falls between March 22 and April 25. **Orthodox** Christians usually celebrate later.

Orthodox priest

Many people go to church on Easter Sunday. Some services start at sunrise.

Others begin in the dark. Then people light candles one by one.

Many people dye or decorate eggs for Easter. Eggs are a **symbol** for new life. Children also hunt for hidden colorful eggs on Easter.

Egg Knocking

This Easter game is popular in many countries and parts of the United States.

What You Need:
- A hard-boiled egg for each player

What You Do:
1. Hold the egg in the palm of your hand.
2. Try to crack the egg shells of the other players without cracking your own.
3. The last one holding an unbroken egg is the winner!

Bunnies are another Easter symbol of life. The Easter Bunny delivers baskets of candy to children.

Everywhere they look, children
see signs of spring!

Glossary

centuries—hundreds of years

Christian—related to Christianity; Christians are people who believe in the teachings of Jesus Christ and the Christian Bible.

Christian Bible—the holy book of Christianity; the Christian Bible includes the Old Testament and the New Testament.

Orthodox—a type of Christianity common in Eastern Europe, especially Greece and Russia

rejoiced—felt great joy

Resurrection—when Jesus rose from the dead

symbol—an object that stands for an idea or belief

traditions—customs, ideas, and beliefs handed down from one generation to the next

victory—a win against someone or something

To Learn More

AT THE LIBRARY

Cosson, M.J. *Easter Traditions Around the World.* Mankato, Minn.: Child's World, 2013.

Heiligman, Deborah. *Celebrate Easter: With Colored Eggs, Flowers, and Prayer.* Washington, D.C.: National Geographic Children's Books, 2007.

Walburg, Lori. *The Legend of the Easter Egg: The Inspirational Story of a Favorite Easter Tradition.* Grand Rapids, Mich.: Zonderkidz, 2013.

ON THE WEB

Learning more about Easter is as easy as 1, 2, 3.

1. Go to www.factsurfer.com.

2. Enter "Easter" into the search box.

3. Click the "Surf" button and you will see a list of related web sites.

With factsurfer.com, finding more information is just a click away.

Index

The images in this book are reproduced through the courtesy of: Konstanttin, front cover; kaczor58, p. 4; kali9, pp. 4-5; jorisvo, pp. 6-7; Radius Images/ Alamy, p. 7; loca4motion, p. 8; Aurelian Images/ Alamy, pp. 10-11; imageBROKER/ Alamy, p. 12; A_Lesik, p. 13; Benjamin Albiach Galán, pp. 14-15; ITAR-TASS Photo Agency/ Alamy, p. 15; ZUMA Press Inc/ Alamy, p. 16; Godong/ Alamy, p. 17; Pamela Moore, p. 18; Westend61 GmbH/ Alamy, p. 19; Kzenon, pp. 20, 20-21; Tim Masters, p. 22.